You Are GOD'S Masterpiece

By
Mandy Everman Johnson

Trilogy Christian Publishers
A Wholly Owned Subsidiary of Trinity Broadcasting Network
2442 Michelle Drive
Tustin, CA 92780

Copyright © 2024 by Mandy Everman Johnson

All rights reserved, including the right to reproduce this book or portions thereof in any form whatsoever.

For information, address Trilogy Christian Publishing
Rights Department, 2442 Michelle Drive, Tustin, CA 92780.
Trilogy Christian Publishing/ TBN and colophon are trademarks of Trinity Broadcasting Network.

For information about special discounts for bulk purchases, please contact Trilogy Christian Publishing.

Trilogy Disclaimer: The views and content expressed in this book are those of the author and may not necessarily reflect the views and doctrine of Trilogy Christian Publishing or the Trinity Broadcasting Network.

10 9 8 7 6 5 4 3 2 1

Library of Congress Cataloging-in-Publication Data is available.

ISBN 979-8-89041-515-8
ISBN 979-8-89041-516-5 (ebook)

All scriptures in this book are slightly reworded for personalization but mostly follow quotes from the following:

Scriptures marked (CSB) taken from Christian Standard Bible®, Copyright © 2017 by Holman Bible Publishers. Used by permission. Christian Standard Bible®, and CSB® are federally registered trademarks of Holman Bible Publishers.

Scriptures marked (EASY) taken from the EasyEnglish Bible. Copyright © MissionAssist 2019 - Charitable Incorporated Organisation 1162807. Used by permission. All rights reserved.

Scriptures marked (MSG) taken from THE MESSAGE. Copyright © by Eugene H. Peterson 1993, 2002, 2005, 2018. Used by permission of NavPress. All rights reserved. Represented by Tyndale House Publishers

Scriptures marked (NIV) taken from The Holy Bible, New International Version®, NIV® Copyright © 1973, 1978, 1984, 2011 by Biblica, Inc.® Used with permission. All rights reserved worldwide.

Scriptures marked (NKJV) taken from New King James Version®, Copyright© 1982, Thomas Nelson. All rights reserved.

Scriptures marked (NLT) taken from Holy Bible, New Living Translation, Copyright © 1996, 2004, 2015 by Tyndale House Foundation. All rights reserved. Used by permission of Tyndale House Publishers, Carol Stream, Illinois 60188.

Scriptures marked (TLV) taken from Tree of Life Version*. Copyright © 2014, 2016 by the Tree of Life Bible Society. Used by permission of the Tree of Life Bible Society.

Scriptures marked (TPT) taken from The Passion Translation®. Copyright © 2017, 2018, 2020 by Passion & Fire Ministries, Inc. Used by permission. All rights reserved. ThePassionTranslation.com.

Dedication

First and foremost, I would like to dedicate this book to my Lord and Savior, Jesus Christ. Without Him, this book could not exist because He is The Word.

Secondly, I would like to dedicate this book to my extraordinary family: my loving husband, Tim; my beautiful daughters, Desiree and Danielle; my wonderful sons-in-law, Travis and Daniel; and my delightful grandson, Ronen. Without all of your love, support, and encouragement, I could not do what I do every day.

Last, but not least, I would like to give a special dedication to my parents, Dan and Debbie. Without both of you, none of this would be possible.

I love all of you more than words can say!

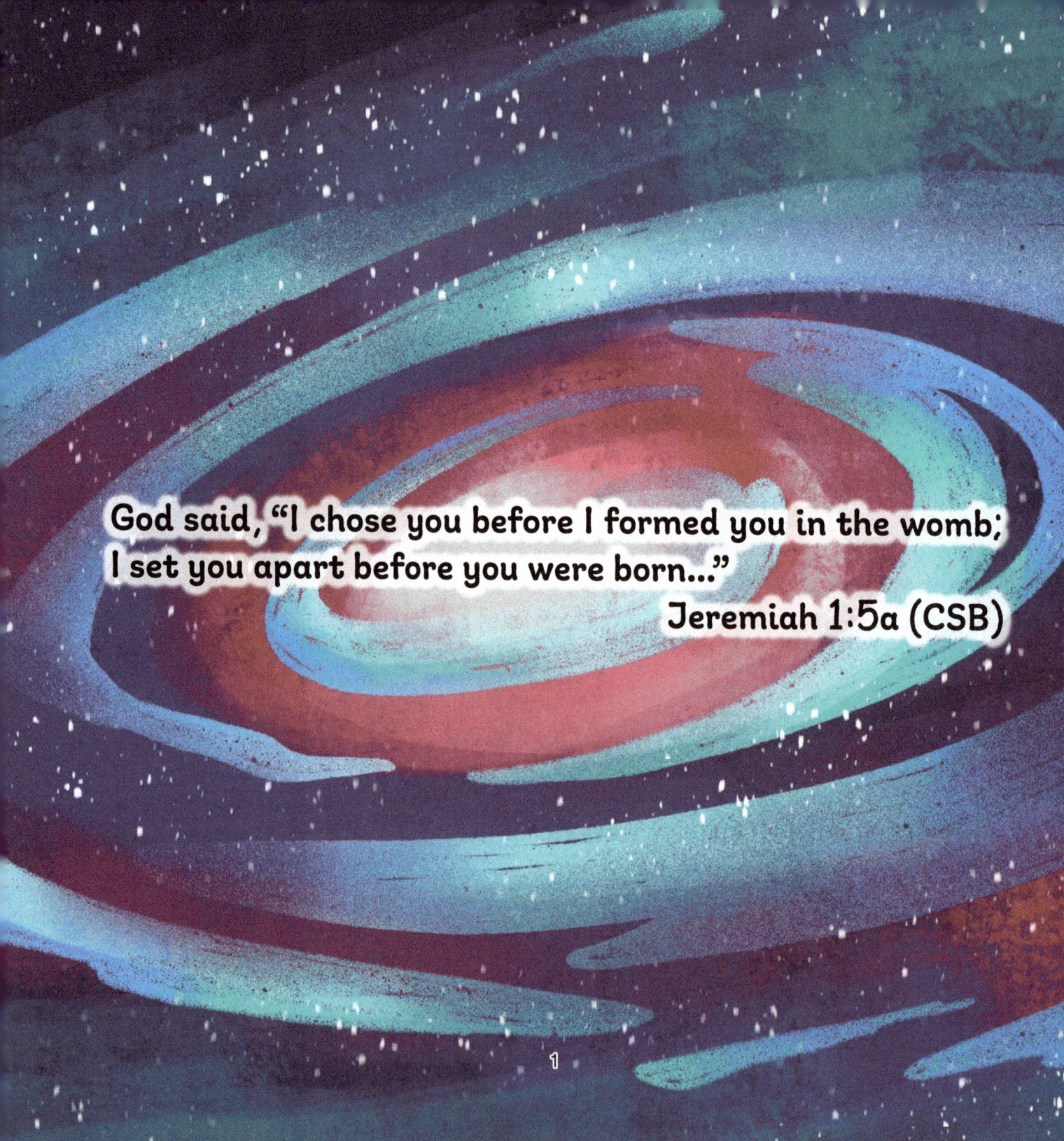

God's very hands have held you and made you who you are.

Psalm 119:73a (TPT)

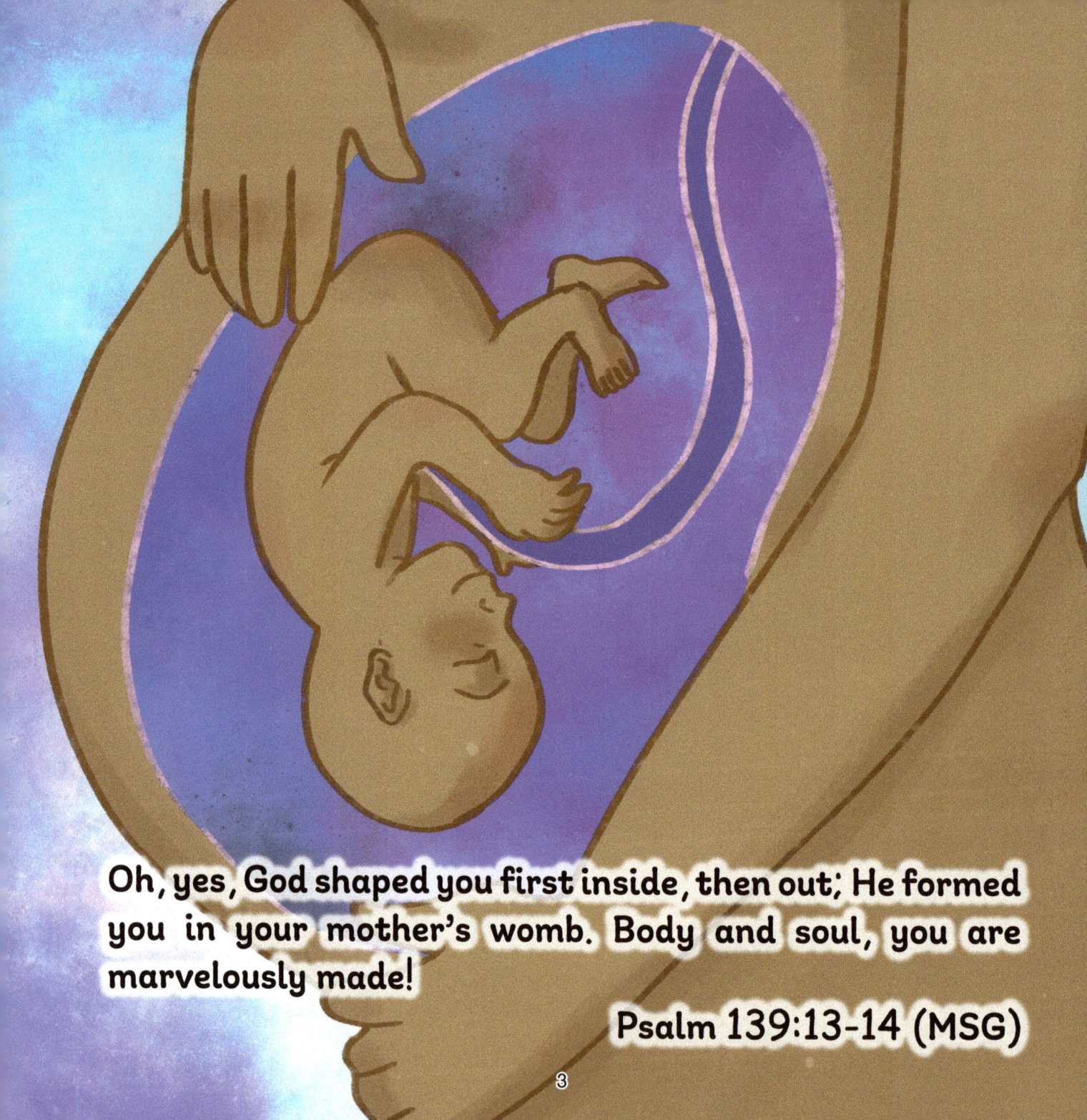

Oh, yes, God shaped you first inside, then out; He formed you in your mother's womb. Body and soul, you are marvelously made!

Psalm 139:13-14 (MSG)

God knows you inside and out. He knows every bone in your body. He knows exactly how you were made, bit by bit—how you were sculpted from nothing into something.

Psalm 139:15 (MSG)

Like an open book, God watched you grow from conception to birth. All the stages of your life were spread out before Him, the days of your life all prepared before you'd even lived one day.

Psalm 139:16 (MSG)

6

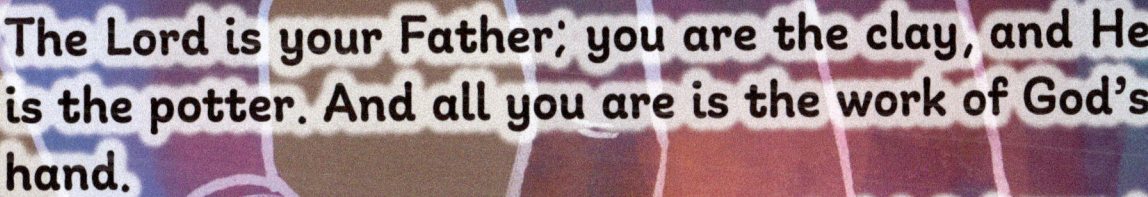

The Lord is your Father; you are the clay, and He is the potter. And all you are is the work of God's hand.

Isaiah 64:8 (NKJV)

So, God created you in His own image; in the image of God, He created you.

Genesis 1:27a (NKJV)

So, you have come to know and trust in the love that God has for you. God is love.

1 John 4:16a (TLV)

What marvelous love the Father has extended to you! Just look at it—you are called a child of God! That's who you really are.

> 1 John 3:1a (MSG)

Every single moment, God is thinking of you! How precious and wonderful to consider that He cherishes you constantly in His every thought!

Psalm 139:17 (TPT)

God's desires toward you are more than the grains of sand on every shore! When you awake each morning, He is still with you.

Psalm 139:18 (TPT)

And the very hairs on your head are all numbered. So don't be afraid; you are more valuable to God than a whole flock of sparrows.

Luke 12:7 (NLT)

The Lord looks deep inside you, and He knows all about you. He knows when you sit down, and He knows when you get up. He knows everything that you do!

> Psalm 139:1, 2a, & 3b (EASY)

Everything God created is good and to be received with thanks.

1 Timothy 4:4 (MSG)

For the Lord knows the plans He has for you— plans to prosper you and not to harm you, plans to give you hope and a future.

Jeremiah 29:11 (NIV)

God has begun to do good things in you. He will continue to work in you. Then, on the day when Jesus Christ returns, His work in you will be finished.

Philippians 1:6 (EASY)

God sends angels with special orders to protect you wherever you go, defending you from all harm.

Psalm 91:11 (TPT)

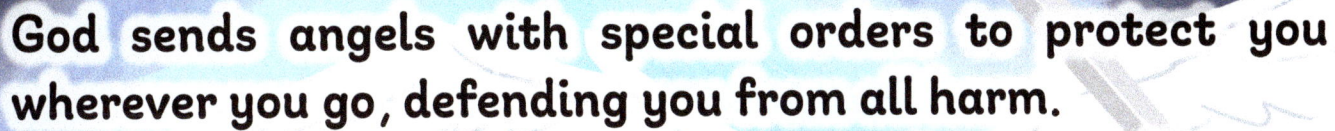

God will answer your cry for help every time you pray, and you will feel His presence in your time of trouble. He will deliver you and bring you honor.

Psalm 91:15 (TPT)

How blessed is God! And what a blessing He is!

He's the Father of your Master, Jesus Christ,

and takes you to the high places of blessing in Him.

Ephesians 1:3 (MSG)

Long before He laid down earth's foundations, He had you in mind and had settled on you as the focus of His love, to be made whole and holy by His love.

Ephesians 1:4 (MSG)

Jesus came to give you everything in abundance, more than you expect—life in its fullness until you overflow!

1 John 3:1a (MSG)

Never doubt God's mighty power to work in you. He will achieve infinitely more than your greatest request—your most unbelievable dream—and exceed your wildest imagination! He will outdo them all, for His miraculous power constantly energizes you.

Ephesians 3:20 (TPT)